SUPERMAN®

IN

ACTION COMICS®

FEATURING THE COMPLETE COVERS OF THE FIRST 25 YEARS

A TINY FOLIO™

ABBEVILLE PRESS · PUBLISHERS

NEW YORK · LONDON · PARIS

FRONT COVER: *Action Comics* No. 25; June 1940.
BACK COVER: *Action Comics* No. 203; April 1955.
FRONTISPIECE: Detail of *Action Comics* No. 206; July 1955.

Superman created by Jerry Siegel and Joe Shuster.

Tiny Folio and the Abbeville logo are trademarks of Abbeville Press, Inc.

First edition, second printing

The captions note the pencil and ink artists for each cover as could best be determined. However, as it was not standard practice to credit cover artists in the comic book industry until recently, this list may not be definitive. While the editors have endeavored to identify all of the artists involved, they apologize to any person misidentified or not identified and invite such person to inform them of their error.

Library of Congress Cataloging-in-Publication Data

Superman in Action comics: featuring the complete covers of the first
    25 years / [introduction by Mark Waid].
        p.   cm.
    ISBN 1-55859-595-3
    1. Superman (Comic strip) 2. Comic book covers—United States.
I. Waid, Mark. II. Action comics.
PN6728.D87S87 1993
741.5'973—dc20   92-12334
                                                                CIP

INTRODUCTION
by Mark Waid

"Preposterous."

"Outlandish."

"No one would believe it."

These were but a few of the comments scribbled on the seventeen separate rejection slips that writer Jerry Siegel and artist Joe Shuster, two teenagers from Cleveland, had amassed in their fruitless attempts to sell their own original comic strip to the newspaper syndicates.

Five years earlier, in the summer of 1933, the boys had originated the strip's star: a superhuman visitor from another planet with powers and abilities far beyond those of mortal men. In Siegel's words, he was "a character like Samson, Hercules, and all the strong men I ever heard tell of rolled into one. *Only more so.*"

He was to be a character unlike any ever envisioned in popular culture, and Siegel and Shuster wanted desperately to introduce him to the world.

They were selling Superman.
And no one was buying.

In 1938, comic books were in their infancy. What few of them had appeared on newsstands were composed primarily of reprinted newspaper strips—Dick Tracy, Mutt and Jeff, and the like—and filled out with lackluster "original" strips starring a mishmash of unoriginal private eyes, jungle adventurers, and funny animals whose names have long since been forgotten. No major character or strip had actually launched from the pages of the comic books, and none was expected to.

That aside, DC Comics—then Detective Comics, Inc., an early entrant in the comic-book field—was relying more and more heavily on original artwork for titles such as *Detective Comics* and *More Fun,* and editor Vincent Sullivan was always on the lookout for material to help fill up the books. Eventually, Siegel and Shuster's tale—of an orphan from the doomed planet Krypton who disguised himself as a mild-mannered reporter—was brought to his attention by Sheldon Mayer. The boys had all but given up hope of ever seeing it in print. But to their surprise, Sullivan not only purchased the strip, he decided to feature the Man of Steel on the first-issue cover of DC's newest title, *Action Comics*.

Sullivan's bosses apparently had far less faith in the decision than did Sullivan. At that time, Sheldon Mayer was working as an editor for both the McClure Syndicate and publisher Harry Donenfeld. Mayer once recalled: "When Harry Donenfeld first saw that cover of Superman holding that car in the air, he really got worried. He felt that nobody would believe it, that it was ridiculous."

Four months later, Donenfeld realized his error. Sales on *Action Comics* were skyrocketing. Moreover, a newsstand survey showed that kids were asking not for *Action Comics,* but for "the comic with Superman in it!" Curious, Donenfeld tested the waters by showcasing Superman several more times. With each publication, sales continued to climb, and with issue 19, the Man of Steel was granted permanent residence on the covers of *Action.* Together, these covers tell the story of Superman.

Joe Shuster's first pencil drawing of Superman from 1933 is a crude sketch, save for the distinctive logo that topped the page. "The Superman"—clad in a T-shirt and trousers, holding a thug above his head while ignoring a barrage of machine-gun fire—bears no resemblance to the colorful Man of Steel we know today.

In time, Shuster came to realize the importance of giving Superman a distinctive appearance and began playing around with the look of skintight leotards, like those worn by circus aerialists and strongmen. Inspired by the costume pictures of Douglas Fairbanks—particularly from *The Mark of Zorro* and *The Black Pirate*—Shuster wisely decided that a flowing cape would help convey a sense of movement and urgency to his flying, leaping hero.

As for footwear, simple boots did the trick (though a close look at the cover of *Action Comics* 1 actually reveals a Superman who wore sandals laced halfway up the calf). And for that final—and, arguably, most important—touch, Shuster added a heraldic crest to Superman's tunic. Though simple in design, the elegant triangular "S" shield that has become recognized worldwide as Superman's emblem took years to standardize in color and shape. Was it big (cover 29) or small (cover 39)? Scalloped (cover 1) or straight-edged (cover 7)? On the cape (cover 26) or off the cape (cover 21)? Bordered in red (cover 25) or in yellow (cover 36)? Not until the mid-1940s did the trademarked formal red-and-yellow pentangle make its appearance, shown definitively for the first time on the cover of *Action Comics* 63.

Like many other covers from the war years, *Action* 63 was illustrated not by Joe Shuster but by Jack Burnley. Burnley, an accomplished sports-cartoon artist, was hired by DC in the early 1940s to serve as one of Shuster's "ghosts." It was not the first time Superman had been drawn by other artists; still working out of his studio in Cleveland, Shuster had begun farming out work to several young illustrators as early as 1938. His reasons were twofold.

First, because of Superman's unprecedented success, DC was committed to purchasing new stories in tremendous volume. Within two years of his *Action* premiere, the Man of Tomorrow was also starring in a newspaper strip and in his own quarterly comic (*Superman*), as well as in the oversized *World's Finest Comics*.

Secondly—and tragically—Shuster's eyesight had begun to fail at an early age, slowing his pace to a crawl. Though barely out of his thirties by the time his brainchild hit its creative stride, Shuster was burdened with thick-lensed eyeglasses and was often forced to work perilously close to his drawing table—often no more than an inch away. In time, this handicap would drive Shuster completely out of the comic-book field.

Fortunately, he had worked hard at teaching the dynamics of Superman to his protégés. Chief among them—and first hired—was Wayne Boring, a student from the Chicago Art Institute who came to Shuster's attention courtesy of the classified ads Shuster had placed in major papers across the East Coast. Along with fellow apprentice Fred Ray and the aforementioned Burnley, Boring—who was to become the definitive '50s Superman artist—contributed the bulk of the wartime *Action* cover illustrations.

Unquestioned patriotism was the order of the day— and while Superman stories rarely showed the Man of Steel flexing his muscles directly against the Nazi scourge, *Action* covers were another matter entirely. Beginning as early as issue 35 (April 1941), Superman frequently bared his knuckles against the Axis, bending tank turrets in his bare hands (cover 44), routing saboteurs (cover 37), twisting U-boat periscopes like pretzels (cover 54), and making one-man aerial assaults against the bombers and tailgunners of the Japanese (covers 48 and 63). At the same time, GIs knew that the Metropolis Marvel was watching out for them, protecting them from enemy fire (covers 62 and 66), providing construction assistance (cover 55), ferrying in Red Cross supplies (cover 60), and even hawking war bonds and stamps (cover 58)!

Only once in the Golden Age of Comics did Superman appear alongside his *Action* costars on the cover . . . and even then, patriotism was the keynote. Issue 52 showcases not only the Man of Steel, but the Americommando, the Vigilante, Zatara, and Congo Bill—all marching straight toward the reader, presumably on their way to kick some Axis tail.

Not long after the war's end, DC and the Siegel/Shuster team parted company. Wayne Boring, who by now had taken over the Superman newspaper strip, split the *Action* cover assignments with Al Plastino, who joined the Superman team in 1948. Unlike Boring, Plastino was hired directly by editor Mort Weisinger—the man who, outside of Siegel and Shuster themselves, was to have the greatest impact on Superman and his continuing development.

Though he had been on staff at DC in the early 1940s before being drafted, Mort Weisinger's involvement with the Man of Steel was peripheral until he was handed the editorial reins of *Action* and *Superman* comics upon his return to civilian life. From that point on, Weisinger enrolled Superman in a wholesale reconstruction.

First to go were the humorous, whimsical covers that dominated the postwar years. They too often characterized Superman not as a champion of the weak and oppressed, but rather as a muscled buffoon who, stumped by the sudden defeat of the Nazis, had no idea how better to use his great strength than to annoy hardworking window washers (cover 98), jump barrels in his roller skates (cover 84), or engage himself in one too many falling-safe gags (covers 87 and 103).

Not that readers weren't invited to enjoy some sensational illustrations during this period. In particular, covers 89, 108, and 116 use color to spectacular effect, while the striking cover of *Action* 101—a shot of

Superman filming an atom-bomb explosion—makes that issue highly prized among comic-book collectors today. Still, it was obvious to Weisinger that Superman's great powers were in danger of being trivialized, even lampooned. It was time, he decreed, to show the readers more of what Superman was all about.

He began by tying the covers more directly to the stories inside, blurbing them with burning questions in order to draw interest from the readers. "Why does Superman help The Mad Artist of Metropolis (cover 170)?" "Has the Man of Steel put a price on his super-powers (cover 176)?" "Can *you* solve the riddle of 'The Anti-Superman Weapon' (cover 177)?"

Menaces became less mundane and more fantastic. No more was Superman content simply to lift cars and bounce bullets off his chest. Could he instead stop the Machines of Crime (cover 167)? What about the It that was terrifying Metropolis (cover 162) or the peril awaiting him on Planet Z (cover 168)? And what of the mighty foe in the alien spacesuit who actually conquered Superman (cover 165)?

In 1938, at the beginning of his career, Superman's unrivaled presence had given him an edge in the comic-book market. In due time, however, his success spawned hundreds of caped imitators. By the 1950s, he was forced to compete amid a growing sea of super- second-stringers for the precious dimes of America's comic-buying public. Faced with the problem of beefing up Superman's newsstand profile, Weisinger took special care to call attention to those elements of the Superman mythos that made him unique. Two themes in particular became recurrent hallmarks of Weisinger's editorial reign, interwoven heavily through the stories and reflected on the covers.

The first was the growing emphasis on Superman's disguise as Clark Kent. Between issues 150 and 300, Superman was shown trapped in no less than a dozen situations that threatened to compromise the secret of his dual identity (most notably on the covers of issues 153, 164, 171, 250, 269, 282, 288, and . . . whew! . . . 297).

The other innovation Weisinger pioneered was an ongoing emphasis on Superman's Kryptonian heritage. Beginning with the cover of *Action* 149, which portrays the ever-marriage-minded Lois Lane studying the ways of Krypton courtship (to Superman's horror), readers were introduced to the splendor of Kryptonian cities

(182), the evil of Kryptonian criminals (194), the terror of Kryptonian weapons (216), and were even shown home movies of Superman's father, Jor-El, who himself had been "The First Superman of Krypton!" (223).

In retrospect, it's a wonder that Mort Weisinger had the energy to shepherd Superman's fate in the late 1940s and early '50s. Forever the celebrity gadfly, he spent much of his time on the West Coast, helping to oversee the silver-screen productions of such DC heroes as Congo Bill (another *Action* alumnus) and Superman, both stars of the Saturday afternoon serials. Weisinger, a gregarious man, apparently established many contacts among the stars of Hollywood, and often arranged for celebrities to guest star in DC publications. Throughout the 1950s and early 1960s, Superman encountered a host of luminaries in the pages of *Superman* comics, including Orson Welles, Perry Como, and even President Kennedy, while *Action Comics* showcased his adventures with screen star Ann Blyth (*Action* 130) and "Truth or Consequences" game-show host Ralph Edwards (*Action* 127).

Not entirely coincidentally, by 1951, the Man of Tomorrow had found a new venue—television. The syndicated *Adventures of Superman* TV show served to introduce the Man of Steel to an entirely new generation of children. Consequently, a subtle attempt was made to mirror the tone of the program with the Superman stories and covers of the period. Of particular note are the tales from issues 188 ("The Spectral Superman"), 200 ("The Test of a Warrior"), and 201 ("The Challenge of Stoneman"), all of which were later adapted into episodes of the TV series ("Stoneman" as "Through the Time Barrier," and "Spectral Superman" as "Superman in Exile"). Like the television show, the *Action* covers of the early '50s emphasized standard crime exploits over science-fiction perils—another trend that, like the TV show, would eventually wind down.

Two more artists were important cover contributors during this period, and both deserve special mention. Winslow Mortimer, a Canadian illustrator who had been working on sister publication *Batman,* turned his attentions to Superman in the late '40s. Though Mortimer's work on the character was at first sporadic, he eventually became one of DC's two most prolific cover artists of the '50s and '60s.

Curt Swan, whose string of *Action* covers began with issue 232, ran unbroken through issue 300 and beyond. A more realistic draftsman than any of his predecessors, Swan brought a quiet strength and power to Superman. Weisinger was so impressed by Swan's artwork that, upon Wayne Boring's retirement, Swan was tapped to become DC's chief Superman artist, a position he would hold for nearly thirty years. During that time, Swan helped to introduce a great number of landmark characters, none more significant than Supergirl, Superman's young Kryptonian cousin, who burst from her rocketship on the cover of *Action* 252 (and, inside its pages, quickly answered the question "Is she friend or foe?"). In short order, the Maid from Krypton became so popular that, from time to time, she actually managed to oust her mentor from the magazine's cover (*Action* 299).

That first appearance of Supergirl in *Action,* in like-new condition, is today worth over $500—and while that may sound like a staggering sum of money to the uninitiated, true comic-book aficionados know that that half-thousand is a mere drop in the bucket. A full run of the *Action Comics* represented in this volume, in near-mint condition, would cost a collector over $150,000. Nearly half of that expense would come from netting a premium *Action Comics* 1: one sold in 1992 for $82,500 and, believe it or not, that was a bargain. Other key issues sought after by *Action* devotees include 23, which features the first appearance of Superman's archenemy Lex Luthor (worth a cool $1100); issue 80, the second appearance of Mr. Mxyztplk, the magical, mischievous imp from the Fifth Dimension; *Action* 100, one of comics' earliest centennial issues; and *Action* 242, which introduced Brainiac, the Computer Tyrant from the planet Colu.

But perhaps it is a mistake to assess a dollar figure for Superman. After all, he is, in a sense, priceless—a unique heroic icon, without doubt the most powerful and wondrous myth American pop culture has yet produced. Preposterous? Outlandish? Perhaps. But beyond belief? Not really. Not to those who treasure truth and justice and, every once in a while, find themselves slyly looking up in the sky beyond all the birds and planes, wondering what it would be like to catch a brief glimpse of red and blue.

Of Superman . . . in action.

THE COVERS

LIST OF ARTISTS

JUNE 1938; NO. 1
Cover artist: Joe Shuster

JULY 1938; NO. 2
Cover artist: Leo E. O'Mealia

AUGUST 1938; NO. 3
Cover artist: Leo E. O'Mealia

OCTOBER 1938; NO. 5
Cover artist: Leo E. O'Mealia

NOVEMBER 1938; NO. 6
Cover artist: Leo E. O'Mealia

DECEMBER 1938; NO. 7
Cover artist: Joe Shuster

FEBRUARY 1939; NO. 9
Cover artist: Fred Guardineer

MARCH 1939; NO. 10
Cover artist: Joe Shuster

APRIL 1939; NO. 11
Cover artist: Fred Guardineer

MAY 1939; NO. 12
Cover artist: Fred Guardineer

JUNE 1939; NO. 13
Cover artist: Joe Shuster

AUGUST 1939: NO. 15
Cover artist: Fred Guardineer

SEPTEMBER 1939: NO. 16
Cover artist: Fred Guardineer

OCTOBER 1939; NO. 17
Cover artist: Joe Shuster

DECEMBER 1939; NO. 19
Cover artist: Joe Shuster

JANUARY 1940; NO. 20
Cover artist: Joe Shuster

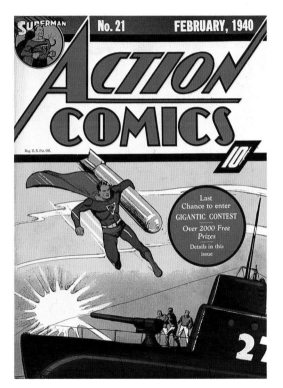

FEBRUARY 1940; NO. 21
Cover artist: Joe Shuster

APRIL 1940; NO. 23
Cover artist: Joe Shuster

MAY 1940; NO. 24
Cover artist: Joe Shuster

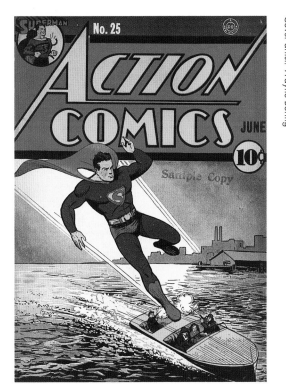

AUGUST 1940; NO. 27
Cover artist: Wayne Boring

OCTOBER 1940; NO. 29

Cover artist: Wayne Boring

NOVEMBER 1940; NO. 30
Cover artist: Wayne Boring

DECEMBER 1940; NO. 31
Cover artist: Probably Wayne Boring

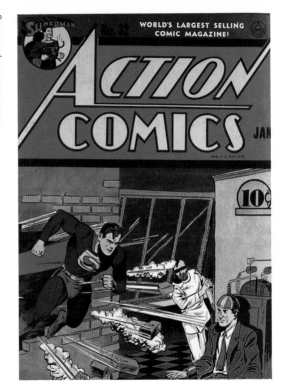

FEBRUARY 1941; NO. 33
Cover artist: Wayne Boring

MARCH 1941; NO. 34
Cover artist: Fred Ray

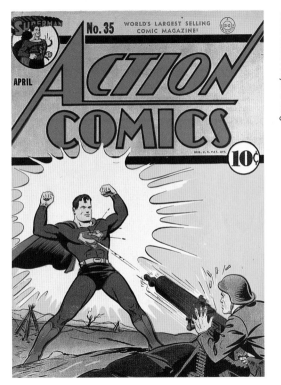

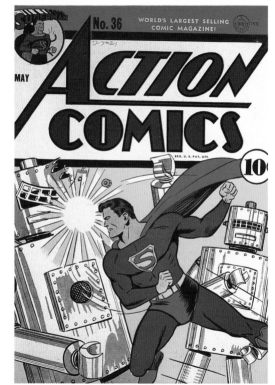

JULY 1941; NO. 38
Cover artist: Fred Ray

AUGUST 1941; NO. 39

Cover artist: Fred Ray

SEPTEMBER 1941; NO. 40
Cover artist: Fred Ray

OCTOBER 1941; NO. 41
Cover artist: Fred Ray

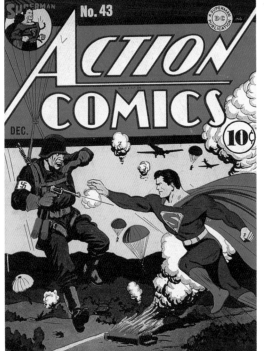

DECEMBER 1941; NO. 43

Cover artist: Fred Ray

FEBRUARY 1942; NO. 45

Cover artist: Fred Ray

APRIL 1942; NO. 47

Cover artist: John Sikela

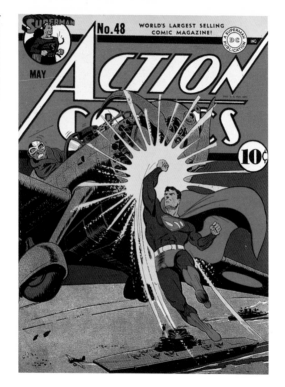

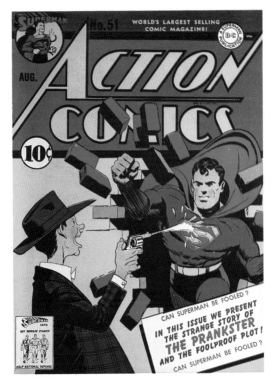

AUGUST 1942: NO. 51
Cover artist: Wayne Boring

SEPTEMBER 1942; NO. 52
Cover artist: Fred Ray

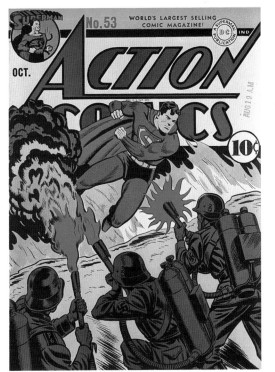

OCTOBER 1942; NO. 53
Cover artist: Jack Burnley

NOVEMBER 1942; NO. 54
Cover artist: Jack Burnley

DECEMBER 1942; NO. 55
Cover artist: Jack Burnley

FEBRUARY 1943; NO. 57
Cover artist: John Sikela

APRIL 1943; NO. 59
Cover artists: Jack Burnley and staff

JUNE 1943; NO. 61
Cover artist: Jack Burnley

JULY 1943; NO. 62
Cover artist: Jack Burnley

AUGUST 1943; NO. 63
Cover artist: Jack Burnley

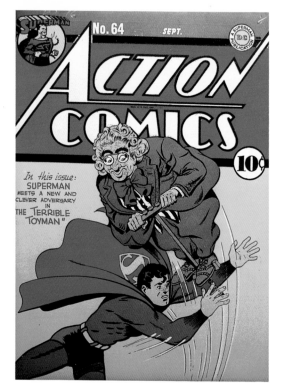

OCTOBER 1943; NO. 65
Cover artist: Jack Burnley

NOVEMBER 1943; NO. 66
Cover artist: Jack Burnley

DECEMBER 1943; NO. 67

Cover artists: Jack Burnley, Stan Kaye

FEBRUARY 1944; NO. 69
Cover artists: Wayne Boring, Stan Kaye

MARCH 1944; NO. 70
Cover artists: Jack Burnley, Stan Kaye

APRIL 1944; NO. 71
Cover artists: Jack Burnley, Stan Kaye

MAY 1944; NO. 72

Cover artists: Wayne Boring, Stan Kaye

JUNE 1944; NO. 73
Cover artists: Wayne Boring, Stan Kaye

JULY 1944; NO. 74
Cover artists: Jack Burnley, Stan Kaye

SEPTEMBER 1944; NO. 76
Cover artists: Wayne Boring, Stan Kaye

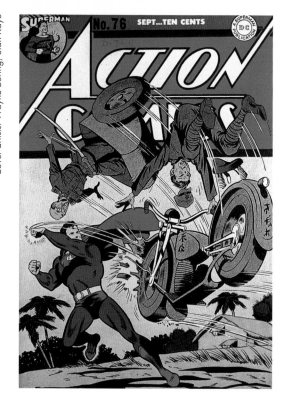

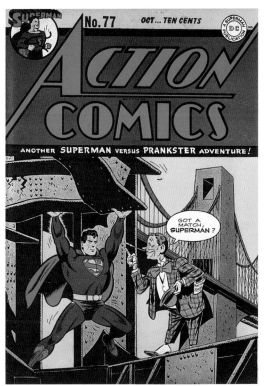

OCTOBER 1944: NO. 77
Cover artists: Wayne Boring, Stan Kaye

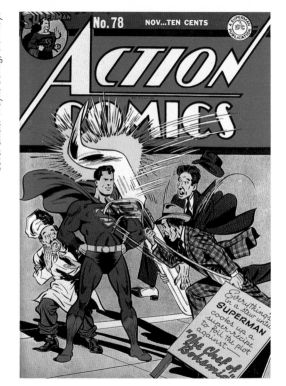

DECEMBER 1944; NO. 79
Cover artists: Jack Burnley, Stan Kaye

JANUARY 1945; NO. 80
Cover artists: Wayne Boring, Stan Kaye

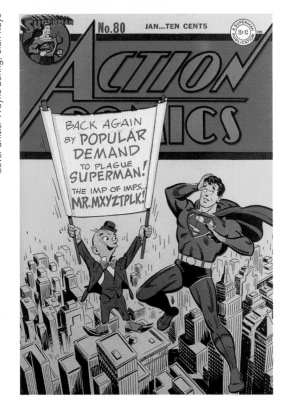

FEBRUARY 1945; NO. 81
Cover artists: Wayne Boring, Stan Kaye

MARCH 1945; NO. 82
Cover artists: Jack Burnley, Stan Kaye

APRIL 1945; NO. 83
Cover artists: Joe Shuster, John Sikela, and staff

MAY 1945; NO. 84
Cover artists: Jack Burnley, Stan Kaye

JUNE 1945; NO. 85
Cover artists: Jack Burnley, Stan Kaye

JULY 1945; NO. 86
Cover artists: Jack Burnley, Stan Kaye

AUGUST 1945; NO. 87
Cover artists: Wayne Boring, Ed Dobrotka

SEPTEMBER 1945; NO. 88
Cover artists: Joe Shuster, John Sikela

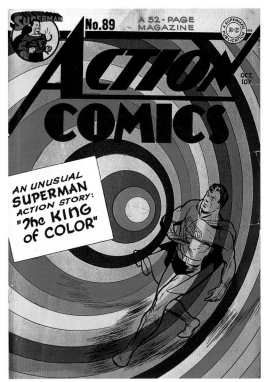

OCTOBER 1945; NO. 89
Cover artists: Wayne Boring, Stan Kaye

DECEMBER 1945; NO. 91
Cover artists: Jack Burnley, Stan Kaye

FEBRUARY 1946; NO. 93
Cover artists: Jack Burnley, Stan Kaye

MARCH 1946; NO. 94
Cover artists: Jack Burnley, Stan Kaye

APRIL 1946; NO. 95
Cover artists: Wayne Boring and staff

MAY 1946; NO. 96

Cover artists: Wayne Boring, Stan Kaye

JUNE 1946; NO. 97
Cover artists: Joe Shuster, John Sikela, and staff

JULY 1946; NO. 98

Cover artists: Wayne Boring, Ed Dobrotka

AUGUST 1946; NO. 99

Cover artists: Wayne Boring, Ed Dobrotka

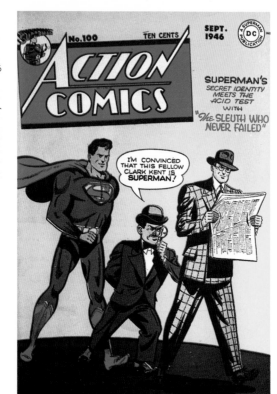

OCTOBER 1946; NO. 101
Cover artists: Probably Wayne Boring, Stan Kaye

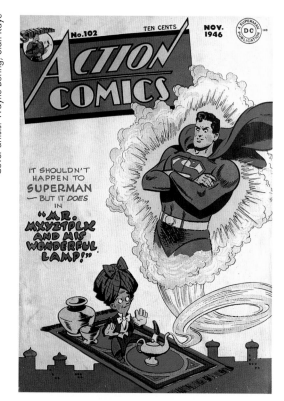

DECEMBER 1946; NO. 103
Cover artists: Wayne Boring, Stan Kaye

No.104 TEN CENTS

JAN. 1947

Action Comics

SUPERMAN
VS. PRANKSTER
in
"CANDYTOWN,
U.S.A."

FEBRUARY 1947; NO. 105
Cover artists: Wayne Boring, Stan Kaye, and staff

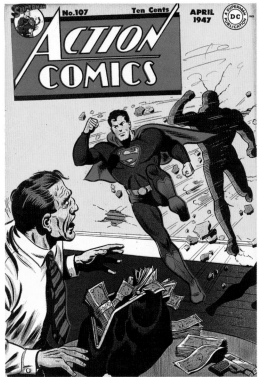

APRIL 1947; NO. 107
Cover artists: Jack Burnley, Stan Kaye

MAY 1947; NO. 108
Cover artists: Jack Burnley, Stan Kaye

JUNE 1947; NO. 109
Cover artists: Wayne Boring, Stan Kaye

JULY 1947; NO. 110
Cover artists: Wayne Boring, Stan Kaye, and staff

AUGUST 1947; NO. 111
Cover artists: Wayne Boring, Stan Kaye

OCTOBER 1947; NO. 113
Cover artists: Probably Wayne Boring, Al Plastino

NOVEMBER 1947; NO. 114

Cover artists: Wayne Boring, Stan Kaye, and staff

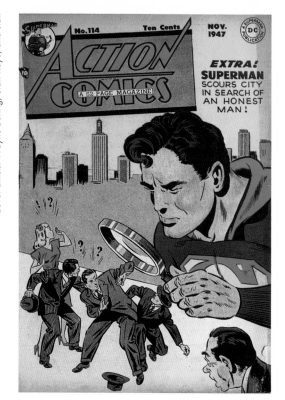

DECEMBER 1947; NO. 115

Cover artists: Wayne Boring, Stan Kaye

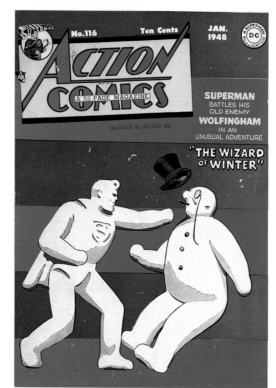

FEBRUARY 1948; NO. 117
Cover artists: Wayne Boring, Stan Kaye

MARCH 1948; NO. 118
Cover artists: Wayne Boring, Stan Kaye

APRIL 1948; NO. 119
Cover artists: Win Mortimer and staff

MAY 1948; NO. 120
Cover artists: Wayne Boring, Stan Kaye

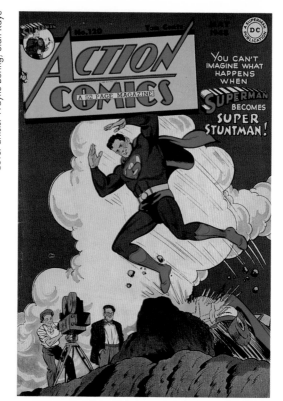

JUNE 1948; NO. 121
Cover artists: Wayne Boring, Stan Kaye

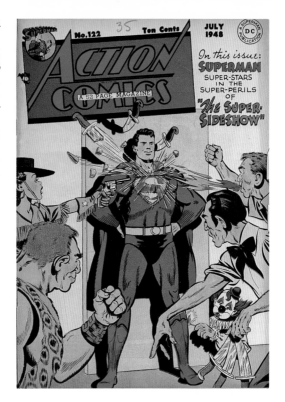

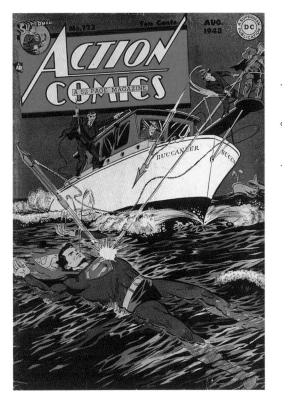

AUGUST 1948; NO. 123
Cover artists: Wayne Boring, Stan Kaye

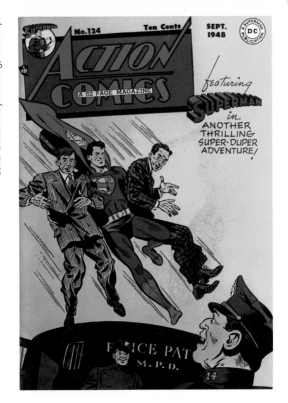

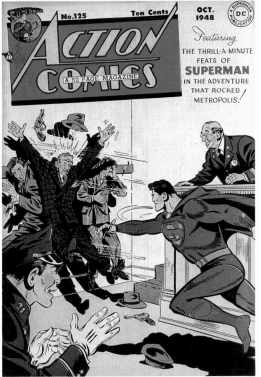

OCTOBER 1948; NO. 125

Cover artists: Wayne Boring, Stan Kaye

NOVEMBER 1948; NO. 126
Cover artist: Al Plastino

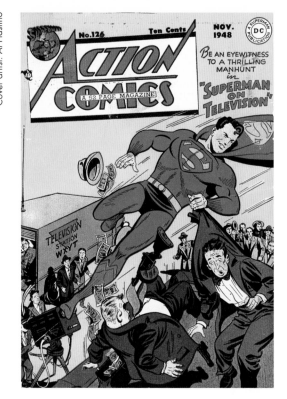

DECEMBER 1948; NO. 127

Cover artist: Al Plastino

JANUARY 1949; NO. 128
Cover artists: Wayne Boring, Stan Kaye

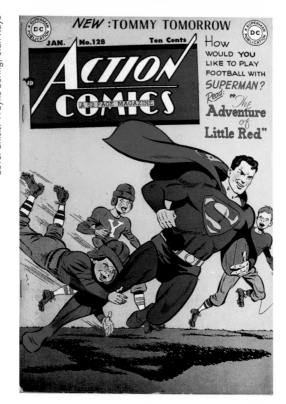

FEBRUARY 1949; NO. 129
Cover artists: Win Mortimer, Al Plastino

MARCH 1949: NO. 130
Cover artist: Al Plastino

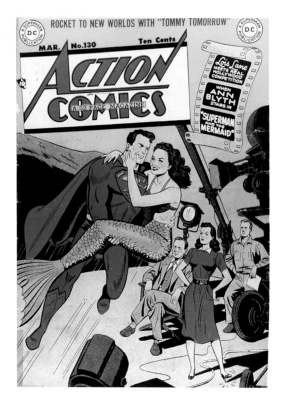

APRIL 1949; NO. 131
Cover artist: Al Plastino

MAY 1949; NO. 132
Cover artist: Al Plastino

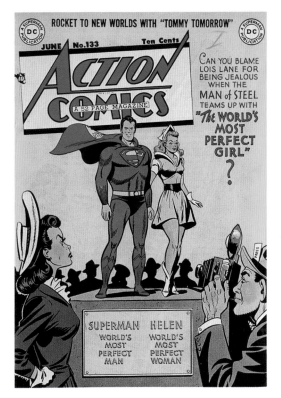

JUNE 1949; NO. 133

Cover artist: Al Plastino

JULY 1949; NO. 134
Cover artist: Al Plastino

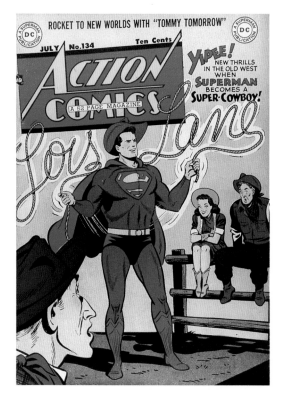

AUGUST 1949; NO. 135
Cover artist: Al Plastino

OCTOBER 1949; NO. 137
Cover artists: Wayne Boring, Stan Kaye

NOVEMBER 1949; NO. 138
Cover artist: Al Plastino

DECEMBER 1949; NO. 139
Cover artist: Al Plastino

JANUARY 1950; NO. 140
Cover artist: Al Plastino

FEBRUARY 1950: NO. 141
Cover artist: Wayne Boring, Stan Kaye

APRIL 1950; NO. 143
Cover artist: Al Plastino

MAY 1950; NO. 144
Cover artist: Al Plastino

JUNE 1950; NO. 145

Cover artist: Al Plastino

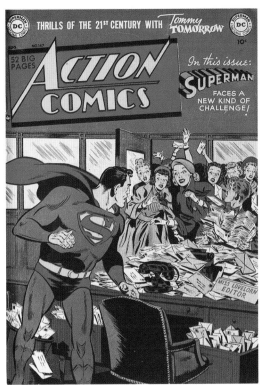

AUGUST 1950; NO. 147
Cover artists: Wayne Boring, Stan Kaye

NOVEMBER 1950; NO. 150
Cover artists: Wayne Boring, Stan Kaye

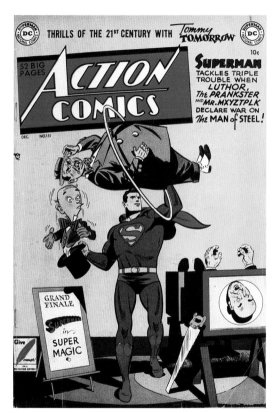

DECEMBER 1950; NO. 151
Cover artists: Wayne Boring, Stan Kaye

JANUARY 1951; NO. 152
Cover artists: Wayne Boring, Stan Kaye

FEBRUARY 1951; NO. 153
Cover artist: Win Mortimer

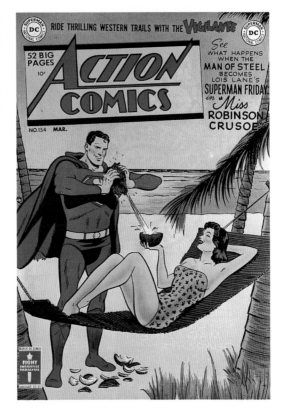

APRIL 1951; NO. 155
Cover artist: Win Mortimer

MAY 1951; NO. 156
Cover artist: Al Plastino

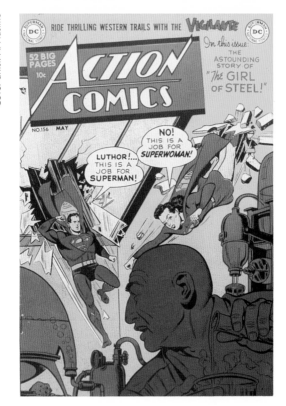

JUNE 1951; NO. 157

Cover artist: Al Plastino

AUGUST 1951; NO. 159
Cover artist: Win Mortimer

SEPTEMBER 1951; NO. 160
Cover artist: Win Mortimer

OCTOBER 1951; NO. 161
Cover artist: Win Mortimer

NOVEMBER 1951 ; NO. 162
Cover artist: Win Mortimer

DECEMBER 1951; NO. 163
Cover artist: Win Mortimer

JANUARY 1952; NO. 164
Cover artist: Win Mortimer

FEBRUARY 1952; NO. 165

Cover artist: Win Mortimer

APRIL 1952; NO. 167
Cover artist: Win Mortimer

MAY 1952; NO. 168
Cover artist: Win Mortimer

JUNE 1952; NO. 169
Cover artist: Win Mortimer

OCTOBER 1952; NO. 173
Cover artist: Win Mortimer

DECEMBER 1952; NO. 175
Cover artists: Wayne Boring, Stan Kaye

FEBRUARY 1953; NO. 177
Cover artist: Al Plastino

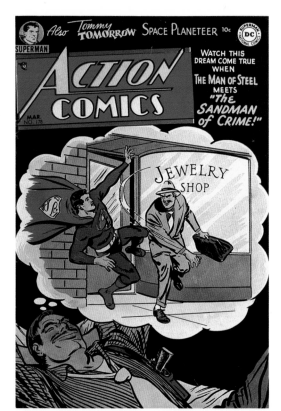

APRIL 1953; NO. 179
Cover artist: Win Mortimer

MAY 1953; NO. 180
Cover artist: Win Mortimer

JUNE 1953; NO. 181
Cover artist: Win Mortimer

AUGUST 1953; NO. 183

Cover artist: Al Plastino

OCTOBER 1953; NO. 185

Cover artist: Al Plastino

NOVEMBER 1953; NO. 186
Cover artist: Win Mortimer

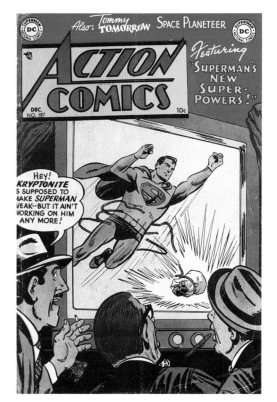

DECEMBER 1953; NO. 187

Cover artist: Win Mortimer

JANUARY 1954; NO. 188
Cover artist: Win Mortimer

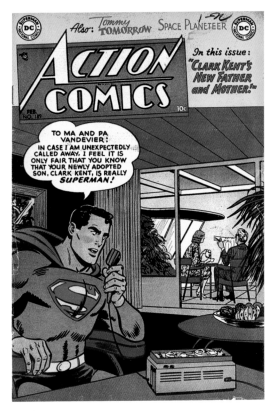

FEBRUARY 1954; NO. 189
Cover artist: Win Mortimer

MARCH 1954; NO. 190
Cover artist: Win Mortimer

APRIL 1954; NO. 191
Cover artist: Win Mortimer

MAY 1954; NO. 192
Cover artist: Win Mortimer

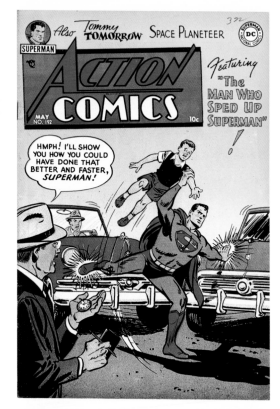

JUNE 1954; NO. 193
Cover artist: Win Mortimer

JULY 1954; NO. 194
Cover artist: Al Plastino

AUGUST 1954; NO. 195
Cover artists: Wayne Boring, Stan Kaye

SEPTEMBER 1954; NO. 196
Cover artist: Win Mortimer

NOVEMBER 1954; NO. 198
Cover artists: Wayne Boring, Stan Kaye

DECEMBER 1954; NO. 199
Cover artists: Wayne Boring, Stan Kaye

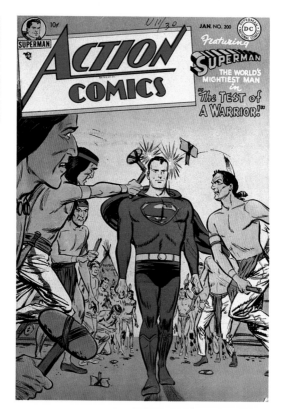

FEBRUARY 1955; NO. 201
Cover artist: Al Plasino

MARCH 1955; NO. 202
Cover artists: Wayne Boring, Stan Kaye

APRIL 1955; NO. 203
Cover artist: Al Plastino

JUNE 1955; NO. 205
Cover artist: Al Plastino

OCTOBER 1955; NO. 209
Cover artists: Wayne Boring, Stan Kaye

DECEMBER 1955; NO. 211
Cover artist: Win Mortimer

FEBRUARY 1956; NO. 213

Cover artist: Al Plastino

MARCH 1956; NO. 214
Cover artist: Al Plastino

APRIL 1956; NO. 215
Cover artists: Wayne Boring, Stan Kaye

MAY 1956; NO. 216
Cover artists: Wayne Boring, Stan Kaye

JUNE 1956; NO. 217
Cover artist: Al Plastino

JULY 1956; NO. 218
Cover artists: Probably Wayne Boring, Stan Kaye

AUGUST 1956; NO. 219
Cover artists: Wayne Boring, Stan Kaye

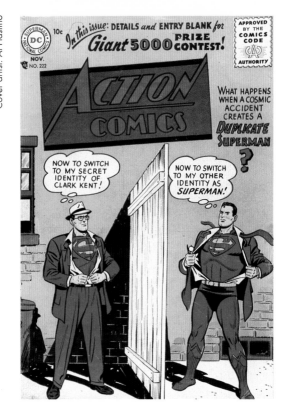

DECEMBER 1956; NO. 223
Cover artists: Wayne Boring, Stan Kaye

JANUARY 1957; NO. 224
Cover artist: Al Plastino

FEBRUARY 1957; NO. 225
Cover artist: Al Plastino

MARCH 1957; NO. 226
Cover artists: Wayne Boring, Stan Kaye

APRIL 1957; NO. 227

Cover artists: Wayne Boring, Stan Kaye

JUNE 1957; NO. 229
Cover artist: Al Plastino

JULY 1957; NO. 230
Cover artist: Al Plastino

AUGUST 1957; NO. 231
Cover artists: Wayne Boring, Stan Kaye

SEPTEMBER 1957; NO. 232
Cover artists: Curt Swan, Stan Kaye

OCTOBER 1957; NO. 233
Cover artists: Curt Swan, Stan Kaye

NOVEMBER 1957; NO. 234
Cover artists: Curt Swan, Stan Kaye

DECEMBER 1957; NO. 235
Cover artists: Curt Swan, Stan Kaye

FEBRUARY 1958; NO. 237
Cover artists: Curt Swan, Stan Kaye

MARCH 1958; NO. 238
Cover artists: Curt Swan, Stan Kaye

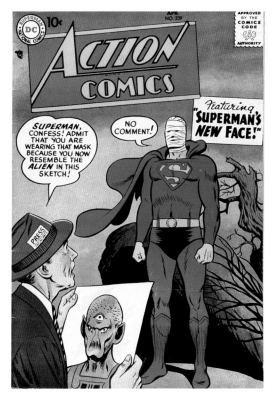

APRIL 1958; NO. 239
Cover artists: Curt Swan, Stan Kaye

MAY 1958; NO. 240
Cover artists: Curt Swan, Stan Kaye

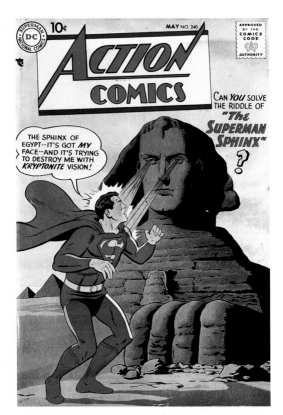

JUNE 1958; NO. 241
Cover artists: Curt Swan, Stan Kaye

AUGUST 1958; NO. 243
Cover artists: Curt Swan, Stan Kaye

SEPTEMBER 1958; NO. 244
Cover artists: Curt Swan, Stan Kaye

NOVEMBER 1958; NO. 246
Cover artists: Curt Swan, Stan Kaye

DECEMBER 1958; NO. 247
Cover artists: Curt Swan, Stan Kaye

JANUARY 1959; NO. 248
Cover artists: Curt Swan, Stan Kaye

FEBRUARY 1959; NO. 249
Cover artists: Curt Swan, Stan Kaye

MAY 1959; NO. 252
Cover artists: Curt Swan, Al Plastino

JUNE 1959; NO. 253

Cover artists: Curt Swan, Stan Kaye

JULY 1959; NO. 254
Cover artists: Curt Swan, Stan Kaye

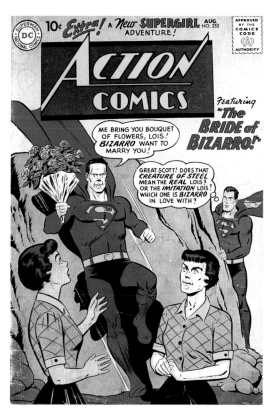

AUGUST 1959; NO. 255
Cover artists: Curt Swan, Stan Kaye

SEPTEMBER 1959; NO. 256
Cover artists: Curt Swan, Stan Kaye

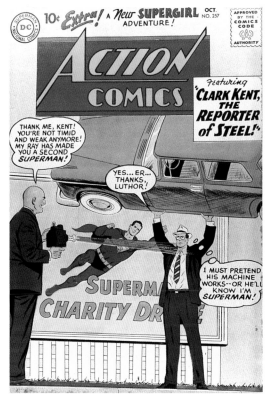

OCTOBER 1959; NO. 257
Cover artists: Curt Swan, Stan Kaye

NOVEMBER 1959; NO. 258
Cover artists: Curt Swan, Stan Kaye

DECEMBER 1959; NO. 259

Cover artists: Curt Swan, Stan Kaye

JANUARY 1960; NO. 260
Cover artists: Curt Swan, Stan Kaye

FEBRUARY 1960; NO. 261
Cover artists: Curt Swan, Stan Kaye

MARCH 1960; NO. 262
Cover artists: Curt Swan, Stan Kaye

APRIL 1960; NO. 263
Cover artists: Curt Swan, Stan Kaye

MAY 1960; NO. 264
Cover artists: Curt Swan, Stan Kaye

JUNE 1960; NO. 265
Cover artists: Curt Swan, Stan Kaye

AUGUST 1960; NO. 267
Cover artists: Curt Swan, Stan Kaye

SEPTEMBER 1960; NO. 268
Cover artists: Curt Swan, Stan Kaye

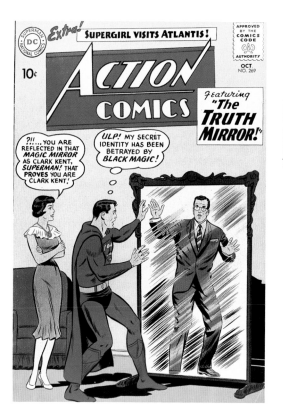

OCTOBER 1960; NO. 269
Cover artists: Curt Swan, Stan Kaye

NOVEMBER 1960; NO. 270
Cover artists: Curt Swan, Stan Kaye

DECEMBER 1960; NO. 271
Cover artists: Curt Swan, Stan Kaye

JANUARY 1961; NO. 272
Cover artists: Curt Swan, Stan Kaye

FEBRUARY 1961; NO. 273
Cover artists: Curt Swan, Stan Kaye

MARCH 1961; NO. 274
Cover artists: Curt Swan, Stan Kaye

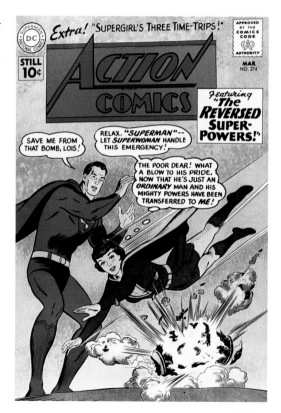

APRIL 1961; NO. 275

Cover artists: Curt Swan, Stan Kaye

MAY 1961; NO. 276
Cover artists: Curt Swan, Stan Kaye

JUNE 1961; NO. 277
Cover artists: Curt Swan, Stan Kaye

JULY 1961; NO. 278
Cover artists: Curt Swan, Stan Kaye

AUGUST 1961; NO. 279
Cover artists: Curt Swan, Stan Kaye

SEPTEMBER 1961; NO. 280
Cover artists: Curt Swan, Stan Kaye

OCTOBER 1961; NO. 281
Cover artists: Curt Swan, Sheldon Moldoff

DECEMBER 1961; NO. 283
Cover artists: Curt Swan, George Klein

JANUARY 1962; NO. 284
Cover artists: Curt Swan, Sheldon Moldoff

FEBRUARY 1962; NO. 285
Cover artists: Curt Swan, George Klein

MARCH 1962; NO. 286
Cover artists: Curt Swan, Sheldon Moldoff

APRIL 1962; NO. 287
Cover artists: Curt Swan, Sheldon Moldoff

MAY 1962; NO. 288

Cover artists: Curt Swan, George Klein

JUNE 1962; NO. 289
Cover artists: Curt Swan, George Klein

JULY 1962; NO. 290

Cover artists: Curt Swan, George Klein, Kurt Schaffenberger

AUGUST 1962; NO. 291
Cover artists: Curt Swan, George Klein

SEPTEMBER 1962; NO. 292
Cover artists: Curt Swan, George Klein

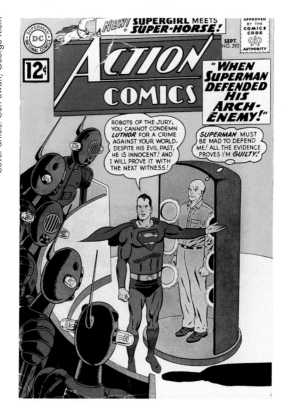

OCTOBER 1962; NO. 293
Cover artists: Curt Swan, Sheldon Moldoff

NOVEMBER 1962; NO. 294
Cover artists: Curt Swan, George Klein

DECEMBER 1962; NO. 295
Cover artists: Curt Swan, George Klein

FEBRUARY 1963; NO. 297
Cover artists: Curt Swan, Unknown

MARCH 1963; NO. 298

Cover artists: Curt Swan, Sheldon Moldoff

APRIL 1963; NO. 299
Cover artists: Curt Swan, George Klein

MAY 1963; NO. 300

Cover artists: Curt Swan, George Klein

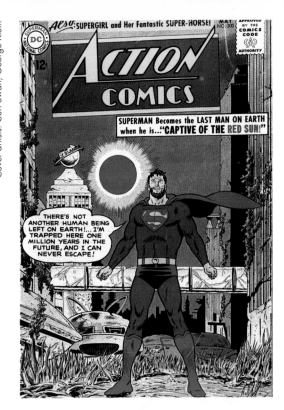